THE IDITAROD
The Greatest Win Ever

by Monica Devine

Perfection Learning®

Cover Illustration: Stock Photo
Inside Illustration: Randy Messer
Iditarod Map: Kay Ewald

About the Author

Monica Devine is a speech-language pathologist and freelance writer who resides in Eagle River, Alaska. She has traveled extensively throughout Alaskan villages, working with Yupik and Inupiaq Eskimo families with special needs. She is the author of *Growing Together: Communication Activities for Infants and Toddlers* and *Baby Talk*. This is her first young adult book.

Monica is an avid photographer and outdoor enthusiast. With her husband and two sons, she enjoys all that Alaska has to offer: skijoring and following the Iditarod Sled Dog Race in the winter, and backpacking, bicycling, and fishing in the summer.

TABLE OF CONTENTS

THE IDITAROD

Every year, brave mushers and their dog teams race across Alaska in the Iditarod Sled Dog Race. The word *Iditarod* comes from the Ingalik Indian word *haiditarod*, which means "a distant place." And distant it is.

The race starts in Anchorage. It finishes over 1,000 miles later in Nome, a small town on the Bering Sea coast.

Along the trail, mushers and their dog teams cross riverbeds and zigzag through forests. They cross two mountain passes and race over barren **tundra.** They also travel over 50 miles across frozen sea ice!

The journey takes them through many small villages as well. In the villages, mushers rest, eat, and feed their dogs.

Most sled dogs are northern huskies. Huskies are accustomed to colder temperatures and are born to run—fast!

Racing the Iditarod takes courage and endurance. The lucky first-place winner receives a cash prize. But in the end, all who finish the race are winners.

Chapter

WHITEOUT

A cold sun shone on the land. Kara Evans stood on the runners of her sled. The brisk wind stung her cheeks.

Her team of dogs was 17 strong. They trotted swiftly along the hard-packed trail. It was quiet except for the soft swish of sled runners on snow.

Kara looked behind her. Not another musher in sight. Already, she had passed team after team.

This was Kara's third day out on the trail. She felt sure and strong. It would take her 10 to 20 days to finish the race, depending on the weather.

But Kara only took one day at a time. She ran her dogs at an even pace. She didn't want to tire them too quickly.

Kara took a deep breath. A light snow was beginning to fall. The dogs were running well. But soon, they would have to stop for a rest.

Then Kara thought about Alex Shepard. He was out there somewhere. Somewhere in front of her.

The past two years, Alex had won the race. He was well known in the racing world. For his wins *and* his losses.

Alex had a temper. One he couldn't always keep under

control. One year, he had been thrown out of the race for kicking a dog.

This year before the race, Alex had walked by Kara's team. "This race is too tough for women," he had said. Just loudly enough so she could hear him. She was determined to prove him wrong!

"This year, I'm going to beat him," Kara said out loud. And she meant it.

Kara steered her team around fallen tree branches. The trail was becoming softer and slower. A Chinook wind was blowing warm air. This caused her runners to stick on the soft, wet snow. She pedaled with one foot, helping the dogs along.

Up ahead, a team of dogs stood at the side of the trail. Two men stood close by, looking about.

How could that be? Kara thought. Two men and only one team of dogs?

Kara turned her head just in time. A mass of dogs—16 in all—was barreling toward her. They weaved on and off the trail, paws pounding the hard-packed snow. The team had no driver.

   8

Kara reached for the **snow hook.** It would hold her own team down. But it was too late. In a flash, her dogs sprinted off without her. Now there were two driverless teams out of control.

The dogs zigzagged down the trail. "Whoa . . . whoa!" the men shouted, waving their arms. They whistled and called the **lead dog's** name. But nothing worked. The dogs veered around them and sped into the nearby woods.

The chase went on. Snarling, yelping dogs screamed through the forest in a blur of fur. One team tried to outrun the other. They weaved around brush, snapping twigs into the air.

Then, in a moment, the teams were whipped into a sudden stop. They wrapped themselves around a stand of birch trees, ending the chase. Held in place, they couldn't move.

Kara burst down the trail. She knew she had to get to them before a major dogfight broke out.

The dogs strained against their harnesses. They yelped and howled in a mess of tangled lines. The three drivers spent two long hours untangling lines and calming excited dogs.

Finally, Kara was back on the trail. Luckily, her team was fast. They wasted no time getting far ahead of the men.

It could have been worse, Kara thought. She'd heard stories about mushers who forgot to set their snow hooks to anchor their teams.

When dogs run off, it can take miles of walking to find them again. *If* you're lucky enough to find them at all. Kara shuddered at the thought. She hated to lose this early in the race. She had spent too many months preparing.

Getting Ready

Kara's family and friends helped her prepare for the race. They packed gear bags with wire, tools, and nuts and bolts for sled repairs. Snaps, patches, and needle and thread for harness repairs. A saw, snowshoes, and emergency food were all loaded into the sled. The list went on and on.

Kara packed her sleeping bag, clothes, wool mitts, a headlamp (for racing at night), and extra batteries. She brought a stove for cooking, a cook kit, and enough food for over two weeks on the trail.

Kara had to pack and plan for her dogs as well. She made special treats for them. Like "honeyballs" made with ground beef, honey, and vitamins. She and the dogs would burn up lots of calories. So they needed good food to keep them going.

All mushers must bring a large supply of dog booties. Dogs wear the booties to protect their feet from ice cuts and scrapes. They look much like the booties that babies wear.

Booties wear out fast. As a result, they are changed often on the trail. Kara needed hundreds of pairs for the race. So Kara's friends hosted a "bootie party." Everyone came to sew booties by hand.

When she finished packing, Kara had over a thousand pounds of supplies ready for the race. Luckily, she didn't have to carry it all.

Most of the food and supplies were flown to the two dozen checkpoints along the race course. Checkpoints are small cabins along the way where mushers must stop and "sign in." At checkpoints, mushers rest, get information about trail conditions, and claim their food and supplies.

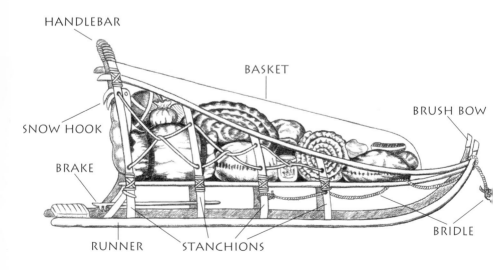

HANDLEBAR

BASKET

BRUSH BOW

SNOW HOOK

BRAKE

BRIDLE

RUNNER   STANCHIONS

The afternoon sun hung low on the horizon. Kara pulled down the hood of her parka. Soon she would find herself mushing through the Alaska Range. But first, the Happy River Gorge. This steep trail could be very dangerous when icy.

Kara anchored the dogs and looked all around. The trail leading down was awesome. It was a mix of **switchbacks** with up and down dips heading 500 feet down to the gorge floor.

"Get ready for a roller-coaster ride," Kara said. She swallowed hard. Then started down.

Luckily, the trail was soft and slow from freshly fallen snow. Up and down they sailed over roller-coaster dips. The dogs leaned into their harnesses, puffing up hills. Down, down they coasted. Legs running like the wind.

At the bottom, they stopped on the banks of Happy River. Kara led the team off the trail and into deep snow.

Poof! A flock of **ptarmigans** exploded from the nearby willows, startling the team. The dogs yipped and jumped into the air, pulling on the **gangline.** Kara held on to the sled. The snow hook was set so the dogs couldn't make chase. But they dearly wanted to!

Willow twigs covered with **hoarfrost** feathers sparkled like crystals in the sunlight. Kara took a deep breath. Were those cottonwood buds she smelled? Or was it her imagination? Could they be starting to burst open with the coming of warmer March weather?

Kara knew what lay ahead. Mushing across Alaska and along the Bering Sea coast could be difficult. Often, there were driving blizzard winds and temperatures below zero. A team could be held down for hours. Even days.

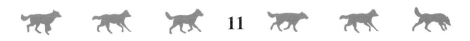

But for now, all was well. Kara was glad for these moments in the sun.

———————————————————

On toward Rainy Pass they mushed. The weather was changing quickly. Kara felt a howling wind sting her cheeks. She pulled her face mask down and tightened the hood of her parka.

The pass looked windblown. Tufts of dry grass and rocks stuck up from beneath the snow. The dogs slowed down a bit, getting into a comfortable trot.

It began snowing lightly. Kara paid closer attention now. She steered around hidden stumps on the trail.

———————————————————

The team pressed ahead. Gusts of wind grew stronger. Kara noticed two other teams on the crest of the pass. Was one of them Alex? I'm not that far behind, she thought.

A new surge of energy passed through her. Her spirit lifted. She shouted, "Let's go! Let's go!" It was her command for running full speed. The dogs obeyed.

Kara felt the wind getting stronger. Snow **squalls** swirled in front of her. She kept a tight hold of the sled. Such strong winds could tip it over like a small toy.

The dogs' pace slowed. Kara was in a "whiteout." Blowing snow swirled in all directions. She couldn't see the mountain pass ahead of her. Or the spruce stands behind her. There was no separation between the land and the sky.

Kara had to make a choice. If she stopped and waited out the storm, she could fall behind. This would be the safe decision.

If she pressed ahead, her progress would be very slow. She could lose sight of the trail markers. They could get lost. But at least they'd be moving forward. It was a hard decision to make.

"What'll we do?" she asked the dogs.

Thoughts drifted in and out of her mind. There seemed to be no right or wrong answer.

Then Kara remembered a **musher's** plan several years back. It was simple.

First, he set his snow hook to anchor the team. Next, he walked a short way ahead and found the trail marker. Then he returned and led the team to the marker.

It was very slow going. But it paid off. In the end, that musher won the race.

Kara adjusted the sleeves of her parka to protect her wrists from the biting cold. At least she was warm, even though her parka had grown thick with snow. And her team was still in

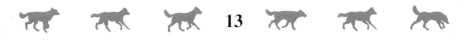

high spirits.

Kara continued on, anchoring the team until she could find the next marker. They moved slowly in the blinding snow. The wind whistled and howled around them.

Kara pushed on for two more hours. Finally, patches of blue appeared in the sky. The haze disappeared and the snow stopped. Kara sighed. She was tired, and so were the dogs.

Another steep rise. Then another. Kara hopped off the sled. She helped by pushing. The sled was heavy, weighing almost 300 pounds.

Slowly they climbed. One step at a time. For two more hours, Kara mushed on. At last, they made it to the top of the pass.

Kara stopped and looked around her. This was the highest point on the Iditarod Trail. Puffy, white clouds softly touched the snowcapped mountains.

Kara sat in the snow and hugged Kiska, her lead dog. "Look at this, Kiska. Isn't it beautiful?"

It was just Kara and her dogs. Out in the middle of a beautiful, vast wilderness.

Kiska licked Kara's cheeks and howled. Both Kara and her team were tired after the long climb. But happy to be there.

———————————————

Kara "signed in" at the seventh checkpoint cabin at Rainy Pass. Then she tended to the dogs.

Kara worked quickly. No time to waste. She watered the dogs and bedded them down on mounds of straw. Then she checked their paws for cuts and scrapes.

Next, Kara checked her equipment. Her sled was still in good shape.

Finally, it was her turn to eat. She dipped a frozen bag of spaghetti into a pot of boiling water. Homemade spaghetti. Her

favorite meal on the trail. It tasted better than it ever had.

The dogs slept. Kara talked with a few of the other mushers who came in behind her.

One had to drop two dogs due to illness. Another had sprained his ankle in a spill on a downhill slope at Happy Valley.

Kara felt very lucky. Her dogs were in good shape. And she was in high spirits. Just tired from so little sleep.

In the days to come, Kara would take short naps day and night. She didn't have to sleep long. She'd nap for an hour. Then drive the team for two.

Eventually, though, the lack of a full night's sleep would wear her down. Toward the end of the race, she'd be running on pure **adrenaline.**

Kara's thoughts turned to Alex. Was he at the head of the race? If not, who was in the lead? And where was Alex?

Too tough for a woman. Huh! she thought, before dozing off to sleep. Her catnap was a short one.

Chapter

TROUBLES

Kara awoke to darkness. She roused the dogs from their naps.

Kara loved to run at night. The snow sparkled under a full moon. The air was quiet. The soft thump of paws on the hard-packed snow made a comforting sound. She stuffed her headlamp into a gear bag. Tonight, the moon lit her way.

Only 45 more miles and the team would stop for a *real* rest. Kara could hardly wait. One long day of continuous, deep sleep.

It was in the race rules. All mushers had to take one full 24-hour rest period during the race. This prevented mushers and dogs from pushing beyond their limits, which could result in sickness or death. Kara would take hers at the next checkpoint. In Rohn.

Deep, deep sleep. Kara giggled out loud. For a brief moment, she almost forgot how her head ached. How dizzy she felt. Her mind floated on a cloud just thinking about sleep.

The trail at Dalzell Gorge snaked from bank to bank in a canyon. Kara knew to take it slow around the turns. Especially if the trail was icy.

Far ahead in the moonlight, she saw another musher making

his way slowly around the **hairpin turns.** Was it Alex?

Suddenly, the dogs lurched forward. They rushed ahead without her command.

Kara gripped the handlebar tighter. She stomped on the brake. But it didn't hold on the slick trail.

Kara struggled to keep her balance. Faster and faster they went. Until the trail made a quick turn to the left.

Instantly, the sled pitched to the right. It crashed over on its side, dragging Kara with it.

Kara groped for the snow hook and shouted, "Whoa, Kiska! Whoa, Nellie!"

The dogs did not obey. They ran yelping and jumping, dragging Kara 20 feet down the trail.

Kara held on tightly. She couldn't let the dogs go racing off without her, pitching supplies and smashing the sled.

Kara dug into the side of the trail with the snow hook. The dogs slowed a little. But not for long. They burst ahead again, jumping and yelping into the night sky.

Kara pressed her weight into the ground. She held on with all her strength. The sled hook barely made a scratch in the trail as Kara was dragged over icy bumps.

Finally, Kara was pulled close to a side bank of crusted snow. She thrust the hook into the snow. It held.

The dogs slowed. Kara's wrists ached from the ice burn. She stood unsteadily. Her right thigh felt bruised.

Kara shifted her weight back and forth to ease the pain. She took a deep breath and let it out. Long and slow. Her body ached, and her mind was clouded from lack of sleep.

Icicles clung to the ruff of her parka. Her cheeks were raw from the wind and cold. But she pushed on to Rohn.

Kara looked up. In the distance, she saw a herd of caribou running swiftly across the gorge. The beauty and grace of the

animals took her breath away. And gave her needed strength.

Rohn was a welcome sight. A place to rest and gather energy for the long road ahead.

It was still dark. But a full moon was shining.

The dogs seemed to sense a rest stop. They howled with excitement at the sight of lights and people at the checkpoint cabin.

Kara quickly claimed her stores of food that had been sent ahead. She melted snow to mix with the dogs' dinner of ground beef and fish.

The dogs gobbled their meals. Kara gave them plenty of water. Then they bedded down for a full day of resting.

Kara took her sleeping bag into the checkpoint cabin. A warm fire was burning in the woodstove. One other musher was

   18

asleep on the floor in a corner.

Kara peeled off her outer layers of clothing. She removed her boots and socks. It felt wonderful to wiggle her toes in the warm air.

Kara placed her sleeping bag in the opposite corner. For a brief moment, she wondered about Alex.

But right now she didn't really care. Her body ached for rest. As she lay down, she thought about her early days of dogsledding.

Kara was 12 when she and her mother moved to Alaska. Their next-door neighbor, Rex, was a Yupik Eskimo. He had run dogs all his life.

Kara loved the dog yard next door. Every day after school, she came home and helped Rex care for the puppies.

Rex made his own sled out of birch. He worked slowly. It took weeks to finish. Rex never rushed or fretted about his mistakes.

Rex was calm with his dogs too. If a dog in his team got the gangline all tangled up, Rex never got too excited. He calmly straightened things out. People, as well as sled dogs, respected him.

Rex knew how to "read" dogs. He studied them under different conditions. He watched them on soft snow. Around lots of people. On fast, slick trails. And around other animals. In this way, he decided where to place each dog in the team—in the front, middle, or back.

By watching Rex, Kara also learned to "read" dogs. She knew which ones would make good team leaders. Which ones would be good followers.

Rex took Kara on long rides with him on the frozen

   19

Kuskokwim River. He would stand on the back of the sled and pedal with one foot. Kara would sit in the basket of the sled. She loved the feel of brisk, cool air stroking her cheeks.

Training Puppies

Every day after school, Kara spent hours with the puppies. She watched them for days before picking names for them.

She chose names to match their personalities. Like Nellie who was shy and delicate. Or Kobuk who was stout and fierce.

Kara talked and sang to the dogs so they would get to know her voice. She let them nip at her fingers and lick her face.

Choosing a *lead* dog took more time. The leader is the strongest, surest dog in the lot. She must learn to pay attention and follow the musher's commands.

The leader also learns to make good decisions. Such as leading the team around obstacles on the trail. Or knowing when it is safe to cross thin ice.

The **swing dogs** run behind the lead dog. They keep the leader going and help bring the team around corners. They have to be able to fill in as a lead dog when necessary.

Next come the **team dogs,** the heart and soul of the team. They run in the middle of the pack and provide power to the team. Kara picked six puppies that she thought would make good team dogs.

Lastly, the **wheel dogs** are chosen. They run at the back of the team and keep all the other dogs motivated. The wheel dogs are the slowest and toughest.

At about ten months of age, the pups were ready for harnesses. Kara hooked them up to a sled and started their training.

Throughout the winter, she ran the dogs over many different trails. They ran on narrow, winding trails in the forest, plowing through deep snow. They ran over ice. They charged up and down hills. Kara loved the hours spent cruising on the back of the sled.

Sled Dog Positions
(Overhead View)

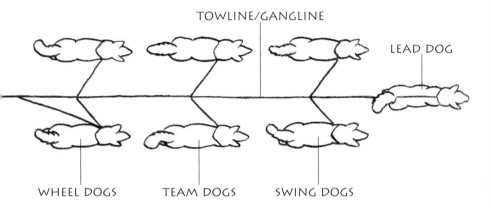

TOWLINE/GANGLINE

LEAD DOG

WHEEL DOGS   TEAM DOGS   SWING DOGS

Within minutes, Kara fell asleep, tumbling into a land of dreams.

Kara was young. She and Rex were running fast on a slick, icy trail. The sun was just cresting the mountains. Morning light spilled across the frozen riverbed.

As Rex watched for birds, Kiska, the lead dog, stopped to scratch herself. The others couldn't stop. One by one, they slid smack into Kiska. Their paws flew out from under them. And the team piled up on itself.

Dogs began growling and snarling, curling their upper lips in anger. In a second, they were fighting and clawing. Fur was flying everywhere.

Kara sat stunned. She could barely hear Rex's voice above the snarling dogs. Red patches of blood soaked into the snow.

Rex set the snow hook. Quickly, he jumped into the middle of the mess. He pulled dogs off one another. Over the snarling, Rex shouted orders. He tossed dogs aside to break up the fight.

   21

When things settled down, Rex placed Kiska in Kara's lap.
Her muzzle was torn and bleeding. Her right front leg hung
loose from her shoulders. Her sad eyes looked up at Kara.

"Kiska!" Kara cried. She groped around in the dark.
"Kiska! Kiska!"

Kara sat up, startled. She rubbed her eyes and looked
around. It was just a dream.

Kara sighed and lay back down. Now Kiska was hers. A
sixteenth-birthday present from Rex. That was when Kara
started running a full dog team. All on her own.

The woodstove was warm. The heat caused her to sweat
inside her sleeping bag.

Suddenly, the cabin door flew open. Cold air rushed in.

Kara opened her eyes. She saw big, brown boots next to her
head. She looked up. It was Alex.

Chapter 3

ATTACK!

The next afternoon brought gray, cloudy skies. The temperature hovered around 20 degrees.

Kara was stiff all over, but rested. She packed up her gear and had breakfast. Maple cinnamon oatmeal and hot coffee. Then she headed outside.

The dogs were still sleeping. They were curled in balls, tails covering their faces.

Kara repaired a harness and checked her sled. Everything needed to be in tip-top shape. She had a long day ahead of her.

The clanging of pots and pans awakened the dogs. Kara watered them and "snacked" them with pieces of frozen fish.

At twilight, the team headed out. Kiska was ready to run. She jumped in the air with excitement.

The trail ran long and flat. The dogs ran throughout the night. Fresh from a long sleep and bellies full.

By afternoon the next day, the wind was whipping across the land. Suddenly from behind, Kara heard someone yell, "Trail! Trail!" This meant a faster team wanted to go by.

"Whoa!" Kara shouted. Her team stopped.

But not fast enough for Alex. "Move it!" he shouted. "Get

off the trail."

Why does he have to be so nasty? Kara thought. He's just mad because I'm still in the lead. I'll show him.

———————

Kara and her team pressed on. Now she was even more determined.

There wasn't much scenery to look at. Years ago, a wildfire had burned most of the trees in the area. They still hadn't grown back. Now there was nothing to protect her from raging winds.

The trail turned bumpy. In some areas, the snow was blown away. Bare ground showed through.

Two hours passed. Kara caught sight of another musher ahead. It was Alex. She had caught up with him. But how could that be?

Alex's team was stopped on the side of the trail. Something was wrong. "Trail!" Kara shouted as she got closer.

Alex was hunched over his sled, looking for something. But everything looked OK. Maybe they're just resting, Kara thought.

"Are you all right?" Kara yelled.

"Yeah," Alex said, shaking his head in anger. "It's my sled. And it's really none of your business."

Kara sped by. She pushed her dogs hard. Why do I even try with him? she wondered.

Kara and her dogs ran steady for several more hours before stopping to rest. Ahead of Alex. At last. Kara almost danced about as she tended to the dogs.

After an hour's rest, they were back on the trail. Kara sang to keep herself company.

A couple more hours passed. And still no sign of Alex.

A stand of spruce trees loomed ahead. Also several steep hills to climb.

Kara drove the team hard. She helped the dogs up the steep hills. Sometimes, she ran behind the sled. Other times, she kept one foot on the sled and pedaled with the other.

Kara pedaled in rhythm, counting 1, 2, 3 with each push of her foot. They were moving fast and strong.

Suddenly, she felt the dogs hesitate. The hairs on their backs rose. Their ears pulled back. Kara sensed danger.

"Gee, Kiska. Gee," she yelled, commanding her lead dog to go right.

Still, the dogs didn't move. Then, without warning, a large dark figure appeared on the trail. It was a bull moose coming toward them.

In seconds, the bull was stomping through the team. He snorted and shook his head wildly.

The dogs yelped as the moose floundered about. He kicked and slammed them with his hooves. The dogs were helpless. The snow turned red with blood.

Kara clapped her hands and yelled. She couldn't hear her own voice over the yelping of dogs. She banged two pans together. The moose didn't scare. He continued to snort and stomp on the dogs.

Quickly, she pulled out her gun from a gear bag. She fired two shots into the air. The smell of gun smoke filled her nose. The moose stiffened and quieted.

Kara didn't want to kill the moose. But her dogs were her first concern. And she would do what she had to do.

Kara waited. The moose wasn't tangled in the dogs' lines. So he still had a chance to retreat.

Bam! Another shot into the air. Within moments, the moose turned and charged off into the woods.

Kara could feel her heart pounding in her chest. She looked around. Everything had happened so fast. The dogs were quiet now. Their heads hanging low.

She took off her gloves and rubbed her face. Her hands were shaking.

"It's OK now," she whispered to the dogs.

She checked the team. Nanook, Marble, Tucker, and Smoke. They were all fine. Blue, Nelchie, Bonner, and Kiana. They were shaken, but no broken bones.

Next, she checked the swing dogs. They had taken the brunt of the moose's stomping. Nellie's jaw was bleeding, and Kobuk's two front legs were broken.

Kara felt tears well up in her eyes. She stood and looked toward her lead dog. "Kiska!" She screamed.

Kiska lay in a heap of blood-streaked fur. She was dead.

Kara knelt next to Kiska and stroked her fur. She sobbed loudly. Tears streamed down her cheeks. She gasped for breath, but the night air felt heavy.

Kara lifted the injured dogs. She placed them on a soft bed of straw in the basket of the sled. She lay Kiska, limp and heavy, in the front.

Nellie and Kobuk were curled into balls of silver fur shining in the moonlight. They did not feel like eating or drinking. They lay limp in the basket, whimpering.

The other dogs were quiet now. After the moose attack, they needed extra time to rest.

Kara sat in the snow next to the team. She talked to them and stroked their fur. She needed to help them feel safe again.

Then Kara made camp. She heated the stove and cooked up a stew of beef and salmon for the dogs. She melted snow for drinking water, flavoring it with bits of salmon. The team had been shaken up. And they needed extra food and water to keep them strong.

Kara thought about Kiska and their training days together. Kiska loved being the leader. Running and pulling were what she enjoyed most. She would jump with excitement at the sight of her harness.

But no more.

Kara looked at her swing dogs. Now Taz would have to take over as the lead dog. Could he carry them safely to Nome?

Kara continued with her chores. Taz looked down the trail and howled. Kara turned and saw a headlamp in the distant night. It was Alex.

His sled sliced by. Kara saw his hand wave in the darkness. She waved and turned her back to him.

He didn't stop, she thought in anger. Her team had just been stomped by a moose. She had a dead dog and two others injured. And Alex didn't stop. He didn't stop!

This is no time to feel sorry for myself, Kara thought. A long race still lies ahead. I'll keep my cool and try to think positive, she told herself.

Kara knew what she had to do. Keep busy and forge ahead.

The health of her team was her first concern. Kara checked the dogs' feet for wear and tear. She rubbed sore paws and put new booties on the team. She knew she couldn't afford to drop another dog.

Finally, a meal for herself. Kara ate beef Stroganoff and bagels. Afterwards, she felt drowsy. She was exhausted and trembled inside just thinking about the attack. Her confidence had been shaken. A good rest would help her face another day on the trail.

Kara unzipped her parka. She glanced down at her necklace. Rex had given it to her four years ago. It was made from a piece of ivory and hung from a strand of rawhide. In the center was an etching of a wolf.

Rex had said that his ancestors believed it brought good luck. "It acts as a protector and gives a hunter confidence," he had said. "Especially in times of distress."

Kara clutched the ivory between her fingers. She rubbed its smooth surface. Then she lay down. Brilliant stars glittered like diamonds in the black sky.

Kara thought over her situation. Kiska was dead. Nellie and Kobuk were badly hurt. They could no longer run.

Should she scratch now and go home? Could she carry on without Kiska? Could Taz take over? Would she ever catch up with Alex?

How did this happen? she thought. Why didn't I prevent it from happening?

Questions. So many questions. Finally, her thoughts quieted.

Dawn was soon approaching. Kara took a catnap. While she slept, a gentle Arctic wind blew in clouds from the west.

Kara awoke to a sky filled with long, gray clouds. The team slowly came to life. Taz was the first to awaken, followed by Jake, and then Hobo.

When one husky thrust his nose into the air and howled, the others copied. They were ready to run again.

The trail was mushy as the air became warmer throughout the day. Kara felt groggy all day. But she knew she had to push on. She had lost time after the moose attack. And she needed to make it up.

Kara stayed on the trail for 15 more hours. During the

starless night, she wore her headlamp. Sometimes she could see the headlamps of other mushers in the distance. She could hear their voices far off in the dark.

Kara knew the moose attack had set her behind. The dogs were running slower now. Was she still near the head of the race?

She looked up into a hazy, yellow sky. It was almost dawn again. Or was it? Kara had lost track of what day it was. She didn't know whether she was in the twilight of morning or night.

Kara set her sights on her next stop. Her home, McGrath. There her mother and Rex would take good care of her injured dogs. The veterinarian at the checkpoint cabin would examine the other dogs.

At the least, Kara needed 7 dogs to stay in the race. But not

more than 20. There were 14 eager dogs left on her team. She would not give up the race.

Taz was doing a good job leading the team. Kara was glad about that.

For days, all Kara had known was dogs, snow, and very little sleep. The backs of dogs running in front of her. The sparkle of ice crystals on the evening snow. A cold sun shining at the break of day. She felt good, but weary.

The team trotted easily over a lightly dusted trail. Kara knew this area well. She was close to McGrath. Soon she would see the glow of the kerosene lantern. In true race tradition, one was always lit at each checkpoint.

The sky was streaked with purple. Magpies swooped down, cawing loudly. They crisscrossed over the dogs. But the team paid no attention.

The dogs trotted on, noses in the air, sniffing out a new scent. They smelled the smoke from the woodstove at the checkpoint cabin. It swirled up over the treetops and disappeared into thin air.

"What in the world?" Kara laughed. "What's this?"

Ahead were signs—large signs—stuck in the snow along the trail. "Mush on huskies!" "Hot coffee up ahead!" "We're watching over you!" they read. They were made by eager schoolchildren who followed the great Iditarod race.

Chapter 4

VISIONS

McGrath at last! Villagers ran next to the trail, cheering Kara on. Red-cheeked Eskimo children milled around and shyly asked for her autograph. They greeted the mushers with drinks and treats.

Kara anchored the dogs.

"Kara!" Her mother strode over, trying not to spill a cup of hot coffee.

"Mom!" Kara cried. Then she glanced down. Her mother's eyes followed.

"It's Kiska. We were stomped by a moose," Kara said sadly with tears forming in her eyes.

They hugged and talked. Rex walked over to the team and knelt next to Kiska.

One by one, the vet carefully lifted the injured dogs. Nellie whimpered. Her jaw was covered with dry blood. Kobuk was limp, but he perked up when Rex stroked his head.

Kara watched Rex. He looked so old now. She hadn't realized how much he had aged over the years.

The creases in his face were deep, darkened. His hair had turned from black to gray. He moved slower, as if planning every step. He talked softly to the dogs, comforting them.

Kara warmed her hands over the woodstove. The smell of coffee mixed with wood smoke was soothing. Steam rose from a bowl of moose stew on the table.

Kara sat down and ate. She enjoyed the stew and sourdough biscuits that melted in her mouth.

As soon as she finished, another scoop of stew was spooned into her bowl. Kara looked up. An Eskimo woman smiled and nodded. Kara savored each spoonful.

Three other mushers sat around the table. They were drinking coffee and talking about the trail.

"Did you hear what happened to Mark Larson?" one asked. "He scratched a few hours ago. Looks like Shepard is still in the lead."

That was all Kara needed to hear. She would not drop from the race. She would finish. For Kiska.

Kara felt much better after a good meal. This rest stop would be a short one. She had a race to finish.

Seeing her mother and Rex had boosted her spirits. She still felt bad for Nellie and Kobuk. And she was heartbroken about Kiska. But now it was time to look forward to the finish line.

A light snow was falling when Kara left McGrath. Several other mushers were right behind her. Kara quickened her pace. She had 14 dogs now, all of them in good shape.

It wasn't too long before the winds started raging. The trail turned bumpy. Blown over with crusted snow. Two hours passed before the team rested.

Kara pulled out treats for the dogs. They were ready for a break.

Taz sniffed willows and dug into brush on the side of the

   33

trail. The other dogs watched.

Then, without warning, Taz let out a high-pitched yelp. Loud enough to be heard all the way to Anchorage.

With another sharp cry, Taz pulled his head out of the brush. He shook his head from side to side. He pawed at his nose.

Long porcupine quills stuck out from his nose like spikes. Taz pranced about, shaking his head and howling in pain.

"Doggone it, Tazlina," Kara cried. "Why don't you mind your own business?"

Kara shook her head in anger. She looked at Taz's muzzle. There were quills stuck in his nose and inside his mouth. Kara got to work. Pulling out the barbed daggers could be painful.

Kara remembered what Rex had taught her. She pulled needle-nosed pliers and small scissors from her tool kit. Then she straddled Taz and held his head firmly in one hand.

Quills are hollow. So Kara clipped the ends to release the air. Without the air, the quills were easier to pull out.

One by one, she pulled them out. Taz moaned and cried in pain. Blood trickled down his nose. Red polka dots formed in the snow.

Kara hoped Taz had learned a lesson. She warned him never to mess with a "porky" again.

The team pushed on. The dogs moved swiftly in the silence of day. Hours passed. Kara didn't see another musher for miles and miles.

She placed both feet on the sled runners. The dogs did all the work.

Gliding along, Kara daydreamed. The dogs ran swiftly and quietly. Sometimes she even fell asleep.

Suddenly, the calm silence changed. What was that? Up ahead. Kara shook her head to clear it.

Dogs were falling through a large hole in the ice. One after another, they slid into the gaping hole. Their heads bobbed up and down. They clawed at the edge of the hole, yelping and howling in panic. One dog went under.

"No!" Kara shouted. She reached out her hand to grab him. Chunks of ice floated around his head.

"No, no, no!" Kara shook her head from side to side. The picture of drowning dogs disappeared.

Her heart was racing. She could feel it beating beneath her heavy coat. Gradually, the thunder of her heart slowed.

Kara knew what had happened. It was a hallucination. She was seeing things that weren't really there.

Kara had never had a hallucination before. But she had heard of them happening to other mushers. When they were very, very tired.

One musher had seen bolts of lightning fly from his dogs' feet. Another had seen an old man riding in the basket of his sled.

At last year's race, one musher saw his team run up into the sky. Then they flew around like Santa and his reindeer. Still another saw bright green pastures with grazing cows.

Kara shook her head again to clear it. She was scared. Was this some kind of warning? Did this mean *she* was going to fall through the ice?

Whole teams have been known to fall into holes. The holes

are like frozen whirlpools. Water and ice churn below the snow.

Kara remembered what Rex had said one evening. They had been sitting around talking about dogs, weather, and winter travel.

"When traveling over river ice," Rex had said, "always watch the dogs carefully. They know danger. If they begin stepping lightly, you may be running on thin ice."

Then Rex had shared old Eskimo lore about winter survival. If a person was alone and fell through the ice, she should dip her hat or mitten in the water. Then slam it hard on the ice. Once it froze, she could use it to pull herself out of the hole.

Kara would remember to watch the dogs. Just like Rex had said. But she wouldn't waste her energy worrying.

Instead, Kara turned her thoughts to oranges. Big, sweet, juicy oranges. Oh, how she would love to have one right now!

Chapter 5

THE COAST

Kara was so close she could almost taste Nome. Only a few hundred miles from the finish line. Nine hundred miles and twelve days behind her.

Her last great challenge was Norton Sound. A long stretch of sea ice that is a shortcut to Nome.

Kara could avoid the sea ice. But then she would have to run along the shore. That would be the long way.

Kara couldn't make any choices yet. Everything would depend on the weather. She had to wait until she came to the sea. Then she'd decide. To cross or not to cross.

Kara ran the team at a steady pace. She pedaled and ran with them to keep her body moving. It was warmer that way.

The temperature had dropped to well below zero. The cold was sharp, piercing. Nothing was between her and the finish line. Nothing and no one. Except Alex.

Two mushers behind her had scratched. Joe Hoffbeck and Jane Kelly.

Joe was very sick with the flu. Jane had lost control on an icy trail and crashed into a tree. Her collarbone was broken. And four of her dogs were injured.

 39

The wind had picked up, and a blizzard was brewing. There was no moon.

Kara kicked and pedaled to make the team go faster. "We're almost there; we're almost there. Let's go. Let's go!" she shouted.

All of a sudden, her world turned black. Kara groped for her headlamp. The bulb had burned out.

The night was without stars. Snow blew into her nose and eyes.

Kara set the brake and called the dogs to a stop. They were eager to rest. They curled up in balls right where they stood.

Kara fumbled through her gear bag, looking for a bulb. No luck. She was sure she had packed one.

She felt around in the bags at the back of the sled. Maybe the bulb was in her emergency bag, which was always packed close at hand. She removed her gloves. The biting cold stung her fingers.

Kara opened the bag and groped around inside. Finally, she felt it. Her hands stung while she fumbled with the lamp. She had to get the bad bulb out before her hands hardened with **frostbite.**

The combination of cold and wind was unbearable. The wind chill stood at 50 degrees below zero.

Kara dared not cry. If she did, the tears would freeze on her face. Her eyebrows were already frozen.

She screwed the new bulb in. A beam of light bounced in front of her. She shoved her hands into her mitts and gritted her teeth in pain.

Since they were stopped, Kara decided to feed the dogs and rest. She pulled the team to the side of the trail.

It was so quiet. Even the wind made no sound. There were no lights around her. No other musher's headlamp to remind her that she was not alone.

After feeding the dogs, Kara got into her sleeping bag to warm herself. Her shirt was wet against her skin from sweating. She was shivering.

It was good her headlight had burned out. It made her stop and pay closer attention to her body.

Sweating at 50 degrees below zero could be deadly. And Kara knew it. The combination of damp clothes and cold air could drive her body temperature down, causing **hypothermia.** The shivering could lead to confusion and fuzzy thinking. And then death.

Last year, a musher became confused and wandered down the trail alone, leaving his team. Later, he was found unconscious. Luckily, he was found in time. Before his body froze into solid ice.

Kara needed dry clothes against her skin. But she couldn't change outside. The cold would numb her fingers and instantly freeze her skin. She would have to change inside her sleeping bag.

Kara wriggled around to remove her clothes. Parka. Then sweater. Undershirt. Then a T-shirt. She struggled against the bag, shifting her weight from side to side. She laughed at herself.

With Kara in warm, dry clothes and everyone fed and rested, the team pulled out into the night. Kara stood on the sled runners while the dogs loped.

Into the black night they raced. Her headlamp sliced through the darkness. They were nearing the ice pack.

Kara blinked to keep her eyelashes from freezing shut. She rubbed her tired eyes with her mitten. The frozen cloth scratched her skin.

The wind picked up. Gusts threatened to tip the sled over. The snow was blowing sideways. So far, Kara could still see the trail markers. But things could get worse.

And they did.

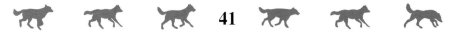

The wind howled all around them. Mini-tornadoes of snow blew in every direction. Within an hour, Kara could no longer see the trail markers in front of her.

The snow drifted along the trail. The wind pounded the dogs. **Spindrift** battered Kara's wrists and blew up her nose. Her fingers ached.

They could go no further. Continuing in a storm this fierce could kill them all.

The dogs huddled together to stay warm. Kara crawled into her sleeping bag and lay inside the basket of the sled.

The sled rocked like a baby's cradle in the wind. Kara hoped her weight would hold everything down. She curled herself into a ball, like the dogs, and waited. We'll beat this storm, Kara thought.

The wind howled. The blizzard winds gusted up to 50 miles an hour. Kara could not see beyond the length of her outstretched arm. The temperature dropped to 75 degrees below zero.

Kara knew all there was to know about surviving in the Arctic. But now she feared it wasn't enough. She would have to gather the power of her spirit. She couldn't survive this ordeal alone.

Kara pulled her legs up closer to her chest. The wind sounded like a roaring freight train. She dreamed of being at home. Snuggled in a blanket. Sipping hot chocolate. And reading a book.

But she wasn't. She was on the trail in the worst storm she had ever been in. Hoping not to freeze to death. Hoping to make it through the night.

The Famous Serum Run

Kara thought of Leonhard Seppala. He had a team of huskies in 1925. And they raced across Alaska too. But their race was to save the children of Nome.

During that time, there was a diphtheria epidemic. This *Black Death,* as it was known, was a killer disease that spread very quickly. Only Anchorage had the medicine to stop the disease. And Anchorage was over 1,000 miles away.

The people of Nome feared for their children. Many of them were running high fevers and having trouble breathing. Soon this would lead to choking and then . . . death. The disease had to be stopped.

There were three ways to reach Nome. By plane, by boat, and by dogsled.

In those days, planes had never flown in very cold temperatures or at night. Planes were flown only in the summer when flying was less dangerous. In the winter, high winds and storms made crossing the mountains impossible. If a plane crashed, the pilot and serum would be lost.

The serum could be brought by boat. But in the winter, the Bering Sea froze into rippled waves. It was impossible to get boats through the ice.

The third way was by land. Dog teams could travel over an old mail route that ran from Anchorage to Nome. It was called the Iditarod Trail.

The medicine was carried from cabin to cabin along the Iditarod Trail. Many mushers helped along the way.

One of them was Leonhard Seppala. He and his lead dog, Togo, mushed through blinding snow and fierce storms. Leonhard never lost faith. He carried the serum in memory of his daughter. She had died of diphtheria just a few years earlier.

Leonhard had to make a hard decision. He could follow the shoreline all the way. Or he could cross the ice pack of Norton Sound.

Crossing Norton Sound was risky. Frozen islands could break off and carry him out to sea. Then he and his team would be lost forever. But it was faster.

Leonhard chose to mush across the frozen sea. He and his dogs battled fierce winds and blowing snow. They climbed over steep chunks of ice. A storm raged around them. The dogs slipped on the ice. The sled skidded sideways.

Hours later, the team trotted safely on firm ground. They had made it across the ice pack. Leonhard rested and "snacked" the dogs.

Then he got back on the trail. Just a few yards from camp, he heard a loud, smashing noise. He turned and saw the trail he had just traveled break away and float out to sea.

Leonhard and his brave dog team made it to Nome. The medicine came just in time. He and his dogs would never be forgotten.

   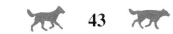

The wind rose to a scream. Kara thought about Rex. His smiling, wrinkled face. His quiet strength. A man of few words. Kara rubbed her smooth ivory necklace and prayed.

Kara whispered to the spirits to keep her alive through the storm. Her body trembled. She was too cold to fall asleep. She rubbed the stone again, creating heat between her fingers.

Soon her body relaxed. The stone seemed to calm her. Give her courage. She lay awake, cold. Cold to the bone.

The light of morning brought fair pink skies. Kara slowly rose from her cocoon. The sled was drifted over with snow, up to five feet in places.

The snow had saved her. It had acted as a blanket, saving her from freezing to death.

The dogs slowly rose and shook themselves. They were restless with hunger. Kara gave them extra treats along with breakfast. Then she faced the pink sky and thanked the spirits. She was alive!

The storm had wiped out the trail. It would be hard for her to find the markers. Kara strapped on her snowshoes and stomped to the front of the team.

She snowshoed for almost a mile. Step by step. Stomping down to pack the trail. It was hard work.

The dogs appreciated a ready-made trail. They loped along happily, tails in the air.

Kara sang. The dogs seemed to like it and stepped faster, pushing her along.

At the sound of motors, she stopped. Up ahead, she saw Eskimos on snow machines. They made a U-turn in front of her and escorted her to the village of Shaktoolik.

Children lined the trail, clapping and cheering. Just the sight of people warmed Kara's heart.

Kara anchored the dogs and walked to the checkpoint cabin. Inside, children were playing cards. Several women were cutting dried salmon for snacks.

Kara bit into a large piece of smoked salmon. The salt swirled around on her tongue. It was delicious. She ate some more while thawing out her mittens over the woodstove.

Kara talked with Jan Griffith, a musher from Minnesota. Jan had pulled in right behind Kara.

Jan was discouraged. She had crashed her sled coming down an icy slope. A musher behind her hadn't been able to stop in time. He ran right into her, and a huge dogfight broke out.

The dogs had torn each other up pretty badly. Jan had 11 dogs left, having had to drop 4 along the way.

Her voice sounded weak. She looked beaten down.

Kara could feel Jan's disappointment. She wondered if Jan would continue.

Kara ate more fish. Then she went out to rouse the dogs.

   45

"Get up, Taz. Ginger. Hobo. All you guys. Get up!" Kara
was eager to get moving.

The ride out of Shaktoolik was spectacular. A mild wind
reddened Kara's cheeks. She pulled down her hood and lifted
her face to the sun. The warm rays spilled over her.

This was dog mushing at its very best. Running free in a
vast wilderness. Steel blue skies. Snow glistening like
diamonds. There was peace here, a peace not found anywhere
else in the world. A knowing that you and your dogs can
become one, if only for a short time, with the beauty of the
land. This was heaven on earth.

"Whoa," Kara called. The dogs stopped.

It was time to make a decision. She was close to where the

sea juts into the land—Norton Sound. She could stay on land all the way around. Or she could cross the sea ice and get to the next checkpoint faster. It was about 70 miles across to the village of Koyuk.

It was a clear, sunny day. A mild wind was at her back. There were no storms rolling in. The decision was easy. She would cross the frozen sea of Norton Sound.

Kara thought about the villagers. They had contributed so much to the race. Hot meals at the checkpoints. Children waving banners and welcoming mushers. Elders telling stories of past races.

The Eskimos had even chopped holes in the ice. They had placed small spruce trees in the holes to mark the trail along the sound.

Kara had heard of dogs that refused to move on the ice. Luckily, Taz wasn't one of them. Like Kiska, he loved adventure. He took on most challenges eagerly.

Once Taz took the first step, all the other dogs followed. They trusted his instincts. And so did Kara.

The snow felt different here somehow. Heavier, due to the salty sea air.

They moved slowly over the ice. The sea's waves were sculptures of ice, frozen in time. Some ridges were four feet high. Rather than go around them, Taz led the team up and over ever so slowly.

Kara pushed the sled from behind. At the top of the ridge, she held the sled back so it didn't bump into her wheel dogs on the way down.

Some stretches were smooth and flat as glass. Then the running was easier.

The sun was slowly moving across the sky. It was very cold. Kara stopped only for short rests to wipe ice crystals off frozen eyelashes.

There was nothing between her and Nome. Only Alex.

She wondered where he was. Was he in White Mountain? Past

the **ice pack**? Did he take the shortcut too?

Bump, bump, bump. The sled felt like it was sailing over a washboard. The dogs' pace slowed. Kara's hands ached from gripping the handlebar too tightly. She pulled off the trail for snacks.

She sat atop her sled and ate snack balls. They were made of oats, peanut butter, chocolate chips, and honey. The flavor of each bite exploded in her mouth. She ate two, three, then four. She was hungrier than she thought.

After snacks, they moved on. It was best to get off the ice pack as soon as possible. Chunks of ice could break off and float out to sea. And Kara didn't want to be on one of them if that happened.

The cold set in deeper and deeper. It was warmer to keep moving.

Hours passed. Kara helped the team by pedaling and

running behind the sled. They were at least halfway across the ice pack, if not more.

"Good dogs. Let's go. Let's make it across by dark!" she shouted.

Far in the distance, she saw something. She was too far away to make out what it was. Another musher? Maybe it was Alex and she was catching up to him!

Kara pedaled harder. They moved swiftly along. Several hundred yards away, Kara could make out a figure walking around in circles.

Who is that? she wondered. She moved faster, running behind the team.

"Whoa!" she yelled. The dogs stopped. Kara set her snow hook and ran over.

It was Alex. Two of his dogs had fallen into a large hole in the ice. Their heads bobbed up and down in the water.

"Alex! Alex!" she shouted. "What happened?"

The fur around his face was stiff with ice. His clothes were soaked. Kara grabbed onto his coat.

"Alex! Look at me." His eyes were blank. Stumbling, Alex turned and walked away.

He needs help, Kara thought. He could wander off and die. He doesn't know what he's doing.

The rest of Alex's team huddled together on the ice. The dogs lay exhausted, their fur frozen. They couldn't move. The gangline was a tangled mess.

Kara looked at the two dogs in the hole. They scratched frantically at the edge of the ice. Kara wanted to get them out, but first she had to tend to Alex. The dogs would have to wait, or die.

Kara heard a loud rumble. She steadied herself. The ice under her feet shifted slowly. If the ice broke, they all would drown.

Alex sat down in the snow next to his sled. He looked dazed.

Kara had to work fast. She removed her sleeping bag from her sled. Then she got Alex's bag. She zipped them together. Without her mittens, her fingertips felt numb. But she was working so fast, she hardly noticed.

I've got to remove his clothes, she thought. I've got to warm up his body temperature. Otherwise, he won't make it.

Kara unzipped Alex's parka and tried to remove it. He fought with her, waving his arms in the air. He yelled something, but she couldn't understand his mumblings.

Gradually, Alex settled down. She removed his parka and his boots. His body became very still. The color of his skin turned gray. His breathing slowed.

"Dear God, help me!" Kara screamed. "I'm losing him!"

Quickly, she laid the zipped bags on the sled and struggled to get him inside. He stopped muttering and lay there, limp.

Kara ran back to her team and removed the snow hook. She pulled her team up close. Her dogs huddled all around him, giving him their heat.

"Hang in there Alex. Stay with me," Kara cried. "Don't leave me now. We've got a race to run. We're running the greatest race in the world," she went on. "Please, Alex. Stay with me, please . . ."

Kara removed her parka and boots. She climbed into the bag and zipped it up. She lay with her body against his. She had to warm him with her own body heat.

Kara heard the desperate yelping of the two dogs in the hole. But she couldn't help them. Not now.

A half hour passed. But it felt like forever.

Slowly, Alex began to move. He shifted, muttering. His face color returned. He would live. Or so Kara hoped.

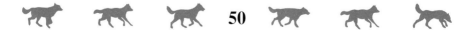

Pangs of fear shot through her. She worried about the ice breaking beneath them. She fought to keep her mind focused.

Then she remembered the dogs in the hole. Kara got up and zipped the bags tightly around Alex. She ran to the hole and stared into the cold, black water. The dogs were gone. Lost under the ice.

Quickly, she cut the gangline to free the team. Then she moved the team out of danger and anchored them down.

Kara looked around and tried to piece things together. What had happened? How did Alex get wet? Did the lead dog fall through? Did Alex fall in trying to save him?

She could only wonder. She saw a hat frozen into the ice next to the hole. It was Alex's. He must have used it as an anchor to pull himself up out of the hole.

Kara looked all around her. Far across the ice pack, she saw another musher approaching. Help, at last.

It was Jesse Roberts. A racer from Crooked Creek. He stopped his team and ran to Kara.

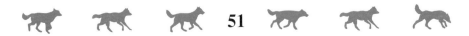

"How can I help?" he asked.

Jesse pulled out extra clothing from his sled bag. He helped Alex put it on. Then he stuffed another sleeping bag around him.

Kara was relieved. She boiled water and made a thick soup broth. Alex was awake now and trying to sit up.

"Hang on, Kara." Jesse said. "I'll race ahead to the next checkpoint and send out a rescue team."

About an hour later, two more mushers stopped. But there was no need for anyone else to stay behind. Kara had everything under control. So the mushers moved on.

The sky was slowly turning dark. The sun disappeared, and the temperature dropped.

Kara moved slowly across the ice with Alex in her sled. She put on her headlamp.

Surely, Jesse had made it to land by now. It would not be long before a rescue team reached them.

From behind, Kara heard someone yell, "Trail!" Slowly, she eased her team to the side of the trail and let the other team go by.

Another musher passed. Then another. Their runners squeaked on the hard packed snow. On to Nome.

In the distance, Kara heard the roar of snow machines. She counted three as their headlights bounced on the snow in front of her.

The rescue team wrapped Alex in a sealskin parka. They lifted him onto a freight sled and packed him with sleeping bags.

"Are you going to be OK?" one of the men asked Kara. "That was quite a rescue, ma'am."

Just then, Alex looked up at her. Their eyes locked for a moment.

"Yes," she said. "I'll be all right. I have a race to finish."

Another snow machine whizzed by. They were on their way to the hole. They would tow Alex's sled and the rest of his dogs to the next checkpoint cabin.

Kara was alone now. She ate a granola bar and drank some strong, hot coffee. Slowly, her energy lifted.

She pushed off into the night. Her place in the race was lost. She was disappointed. But at the same time, her desire to win had lost its power over her.

Finally, they made it to land. Kara's team charged ahead in the darkness. No wind, no snow. Just a cold, clean night.

The shoreline stretched out far in front of her. Kara met every curve of the trail like an old friend.

Kara looked up and stopped the team. A burst of shining, green lights filled the night sky. The lights turned white, then green again. They shimmered and danced in the darkness. In the silence, she heard crackling sounds. Kara sat on her sled and watched the show of **northern lights.**

Along Front Street, people waved and cheered as Kara mushed into Nome. It was 5 a.m. The air was still and cold. Cameras flashed, and journalists buzzed around her. They asked many questions about the rescue. She shook people's hands and signed autographs.

Then she tended to her dogs. They were the real heroes of the race. After watering and feeding them, she hugged each one.

"Kiska would be so proud of you guys," Kara said to the team. "And so am I."

Kara ate a huge breakfast. Eggs, hash brown potatoes, sourdough pancakes, and caribou sausage.

Now that the race was over, the pressure was gone. She looked forward to a shower and sleep. Lots of it.

Days later, Kara received the "Spirit of Iditarod" Award for the courage and compassion she showed during the race. Her lifesaving efforts would never be forgotten. Especially by Alex.

In a letter from his hospital bed, Alex wrote:

"Thank you for saving my life. I guess it takes more than being tough to win a race. I hope to see you on the trail again next year."

Kara folded the letter. Hers *was* the greatest win ever. To save a life.

Next year, she'd be back. Back on the Iditarod Trail.

GLOSSARY

- **adrenaline**   a chemical in the body that provides extra energy and endurance

- **frostbite**   when a part of the body is injured from intense cold. Usually the fingers and toes are affected.

- **gangline**   the main line or rope to which all the dogs are connected. Each dog is connected to the gangline by a tugline (at the back of the harness) and a neckline (which is attached to the dog's collar).

- **hairpin turns**   a U-shaped turn in the trail, like a hairpin

- **hoarfrost**   the ice crystals that form when moist air hits a frozen surface

- **hypothermia**   hypothermia means "too little heat" and happens when your body temperature drops below normal.

- **ice pack**   large masses of ice frozen together. The Norton Sound ice pack is a long arm of the sea that juts into the land. Mushers cross the ice pack on their way to Nome.

- **lead dog**   the dog at the head of the team. The other team dogs are lined out behind the leader.

- **musher**   a person who travels on foot over snow with a dogsled. The command *mush!* is often used to tell the dogs to go faster.

- **northern lights** green and pink streaks of light that shimmer and dance in the night sky. They are caused by hot gases from the sun that get trapped in the earth's magnetic field.

- **ptarmigan** a small grouse that is the Alaska state bird. In the summer, its feathers are brown, and in the winter, its feathers are fluffy white.

- **snow hook** (or **sled hook**) a heavy metal hook that is used to hold the team in place. The hook is thrust deep into the snow to anchor the dogs.

- **spindrift** a spray of fine snow blown by the wind

- **squalls** a sudden snowstorm with very strong winds

- **swing dogs** the dogs directly behind the leader that help to steer the team around corners

- **switchback** a steep trail following a zigzag course

- **team dogs** the team dogs run directly behind the swing dogs. They provide speed and power to the team.

- **tundra** the tundra is low, flat land that stretches for miles and miles in northern Alaska. Beneath the tundra, the ground stays frozen all year round.

- **wheel dogs** the last two dogs that are closest to the sled. The wheel dogs are usually the largest and strongest dogs of the team.